RANDOM ACTS OF MANAGEMENT

Other DILBERT books from Andrews McMeel Publishing

Dilbert Gives You the Business
ISBN: 0-7407-0338-2 hardcover
ISBN: 0-7407-0003-0 paperback

Don't Step in the Leadership
ISBN: 0-8362-7844-5

Journey to Cubeville
ISBN: 0-8362-7175-0 hardcover
ISBN: 0-8362-6745-1 paperback

I'm Not Anti-Business, I'm Anti-Idiot
ISBN: 0-8362-5182-2

Seven Years of Highly Defective People
ISBN: 0-8392-5129-6 hardcover
ISBN: 0-8362-3668-8 paperback

Casual Day Has Gone Too Far
ISBN: 0-8362-2899-5

Fugitive from the Cubicle Police
ISBN: 0-8362-2119-2

Still Pumped from Using the Mouse
ISBN: 0-8362-1026-3

It's Obvious You Won't Survive by Your Wits Alone
ISBN: 0-8362-0415-8

Bring Me the Head of Willy the Mailboy!
ISBN: 0-8362-1779-9

Shave the Whales
ISBN: 0-8362-1740-3

Dogbert's Clues for the Clueless
ISBN: 0-8362-1737-3

Build a Better Life by Stealing Office Supplies
ISBN: 0-8362-1757-8

Always Postpone Meetings with Time-Wasting Morons
ISBN: 0-8362-1758-6

For ordering information, call 1-800-642-6480.

RANDOM ACTS OF MANAGEMENT

A DILBERT® BOOK

BY **SCOTT ADAMS**

Andrews McMeel
Publishing

Kansas City

00 01 02 03 04 BAH 10 9 8 7 6 5 4 3 2 1

ISBN: 0-7407-0453-2

Library of Congress Catalog Card Number: 99-68659

For Smokey's favorite

Introduction

I keep reading stories about CEOs of large companies who make hundreds of millions of dollars in stock options. There is some debate as to whether this is appropriate. One argument is that these CEOs are visionaries, uniquely qualified to create spectacular stockholder value. Another possibility is that CEOs are just showing up and shuffling things around until something lucky happens. I'm leaning toward the "showing up and shuffling" theory.

I'm not saying CEOs are dumb. Put yourself in their shoes. When you're a CEO the only information you have is what your subordinates give you. And they're all unscrupulous sycophants. The last thing you'd ever hear is the truth. So there you are, a powerful CEO astride some mammoth enterprise, armed with no useful information whatsoever. You know you have to do something but there's no way to know what. Your only rational strategy is to do random things until something lucky happens, then take credit.

The alternative—acting nonrandomly—is a sure loser. Let's say, for example, you're a CEO and you fire everyone whose last name starts with the letter *M*. That's a clear pattern, and not a good one. Everyone would think you were a nut. You see, when you don't have a good strategy, any activity that looks like a pattern just makes you look bad.

Conversely, if you act randomly, reorganizing for no particular reason, promoting idiots, merging unrelated businesses, spinning off a few divisions—that looks like leadership. It's leadership for the simple reason that your employees never would have made those changes on their own. Later, when something lucky happens, you can take credit. If nothing lucky happens, call it a transition period.

I wonder what CEOs say to their spouses in private. Do the CEOs begin to believe that their management decisions are connected to the results? I bet they do. It probably sounds like this:

CEO: "Honey, I fired my VP of marketing because I didn't like his shirt, and our stock went up a point!"

Spouse: "Didn't the Fed lower interest rates today?"

CEO: "Try to stay on the topic."

Speaking of other topics, you can still join Dogbert's New Ruling Class (DNRC) and receive the free *Dilbert* newsletter whenever I feel like it, which turns out to be about three or four times a year. When Dogbert conquers the earth, those not on the list will become our domestic servants, except for the CEOs, who have no useful skills.

To subscribe, send a blank E-mail to dilbert-text-on@list.unitedmedia.com.
To unsubscribe, send a blank E-mail to dilbert-off@list.unitedmedia.com.
If you have problems with the automated subscription method, write to newsletter@unitedmedia.com.

You can also subscribe via snail mail:

Dilbert Mailing List
United Media
200 Madison Ave.
New York, NY 10016

S. Adams

Scott Adams

12

15

18

YOU EXPECT ME TO SIGN THIS? THE LEGALESE IS TOTALLY INCOMPREHENSIBLE.

YOU WILL.

DO YOU EXPECT ME TO GIVE UP LEGAL RIGHTS JUST BECAUSE IT'S TOO HARD TO FIGURE OUT WHAT ANY OF IT MEANS?

YES.

AND INITIAL THE "INVOLUNTARY BIOLOGICAL TESTING" BOX.

OKAY, OKAY!

OUR NEW LINE OF BUSINESS IS TESTING EXPERIMENTAL MEDICAL PROCEDURES ON EMPLOYEES.

TODAY'S TEST IS CALLED THE UNICORN ANTIDEPRESSANT THERAPY.

ACCORDING TO THE INSTRUCTIONS, IN A FEW MINUTES, I'LL SEE SOMETHING THAT WILL MAKE ME LAUGH.

LATELY, I'VE BEEN GROWING A UNICORN HORN.

IN SOME CULTURES, THIS WOULD BE A SIGN OF GREAT VIRILITY.

IT'S TIME TO ADMIT THAT I DON'T KNOW WHAT WOMEN WANT.

21

JOB COUNSELING

WE'LL NEED TO DISGUISE THE FACT THAT YOU'RE A MORON.

IRONICALLY, THE BEST WAY IS TO BECOME AN EXPERT IN SOMETHING CALLED "KNOWLEDGE MANAGEMENT."

WE MUST DEVELOP KNOWLEDGE OPTIMIZATION INITIATIVES TO LEVERAGE OUR KEY LEARNINGS.

SMART.

THEN WE NEED TO PV THE DCF AND GET THE ROI TO THE EOC ASAP.

ARE YOU OUR NEW CFO OR A BABBLING IDIOT WHO JUST HAPPENED TO WANDER BY?

WHICH ONE PAYS MORE?

THE MYSTERY DEEPENS.

CHIEF FINANCIAL OFFICER

I NEED ONE-SENTENCE DESCRIPTIONS OF EACH OF YOUR PROJECTS.

YOU'RE PLANNING TO MAKE CRITICAL BUDGET DECISIONS BASED ON THAT?

YES.

WOW. FIVE PAGES WITHOUT USING A PERIOD.

THANK GOD FOR SEMI-COLONS.

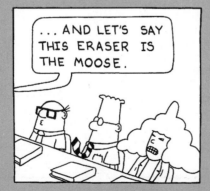

WALLY, MAY I TAP IN TO YOUR VAST WISDOM?

OKAY, BUT MAKE SURE YOU PULL OUT BEFORE YOUR HEAD EXPLODES.

I'VE NOTICED THAT MANY EMPLOYEES ARE EVIL, SADISTIC OBSTRUCTIONISTS.

DO ALL THE NUTS WORK HERE BY SOME STRANGE COINCIDENCE?

OR ARE MOST EMPLOYEES EVIL?

DON'T FOCUS ON THE EVIL, ASOK.

© 1998 United Feature Syndicate, Inc.

FOCUS ON THE FEW EMPLOYEES WHO SEEM GOOD.

THEY'RE THE ONES WHO WILL STAB YOU WHEN YOU'RE SLEEPING!

TRUST NO ONE BUT THE LAZY!

OW! OW! OW!

I WARNED YOU TO PULL OUT!

30

Panel 1: I CREATED A COMPLEX FINANCIAL MODEL FOR OUR COMPANY.

LET'S SEE.

Panel 2: IT'S DANGEROUS IF YOU DON'T UNDERSTAND IT.

THAT'S WHAT THEY TOLD LINDBERGH...

Panel 3: BUT THAT DIDN'T STOP HIM FROM INVENTING THE LIGHTBULB.

Panel 4: I DID SOME FINANCIAL MODELING ON MY OWN.

Panel 5: BUT YOU DON'T KNOW ANY OF THE ASSUMPTIONS THAT WENT INTO THE ORIGINAL SPREAD-SHEET.

Panel 6: THAT DIDN'T STOP ME FROM DEVELOPING A STRATEGY.

OUR PAY IS BASED ON THE TAX RATE NOW.

Panel 7: NOTHING IS MORE DANGEROUS THAN A BOSS WITH A SPREADSHEET.

Panel 8: IF I INCREASE THE PAGE NUMBER, OUR SALES GO UP.

I'M ONTO SOMETHING.

Panel 9: ON PAGE 843 THE SALES WOULD BE HIGHER, BUT I WAS EXHAUSTED.

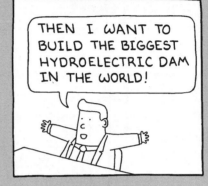

I'M CHATTING WITH A SUPERMODEL WHO HAS TROUBLE FINDING DATES.

SHE SAYS MEN ARE INTIMIDATED BY HER BEAUTY AND HER COMPUTER SKILLS.

DANG! THE SYSTEM ADMINISTRATOR IS MAKING A MOVE ON HER.

TYPE FASTER!

I SET UP A DATE WITH THE SUPER-MODEL I MET ON THE INTERNET.

SUPERMODELS DON'T LOOK GOOD IN PERSON.

THAT'S SILLY.

I DON'T KNOW HOW TO USE A VASE. DO YOU MIND IF I THROW THOSE IN THE TRASH?

DATING A SUPERMODEL

I HEAR THE CAMERA ADDS...UM... EIGHTY POUNDS?

YES. AND IF YOU USE BLACK AND WHITE FILM, THE CAMERA ADDS MAKEUP TOO.

DOES THE CAMERA ADD HAIR?

WHY WOULD IT NEED TO?

I'LL HAVE THE JUMBO SPAGHETTI MEAL WITH A LOAF OF GARLIC BREAD.

I'LL ABSORB MOISTURE FROM THE AIR AND SNIFF THE MINTS ON THE WAY OUT.

IS IT FUN TO BE A SUPER-MODEL?

IT WAS UNTIL NOW.

I REALIZE WE'RE FROM DIFFERENT WORLDS, BONITA.

YOU'RE A FAMOUS SUPERMODEL AND I'M JUST A SEXY ENGINEER...

BUT WHEN I GAZE INTO YOUR... UM... EYE SOCKETS...

GOOD NIGHT.

WE MUST MAINTAIN A SENSE OF URGENCY. SPEED IS THE KEY. WE MUST BE FASTER THAN THE COMPETITION.

DOES THAT MEAN YOU'LL SIGN THE STUFF THAT'S BEEN ON YOUR DESK FOR A MONTH?

LOGICAL QUESTIONS DON'T MIX WITH MOTIVATIONAL MESSAGES.

CATBERT THE DIRECTOR OF HUMAN RESOURCES

SO, YOU WANT A JOB HERE, TUBBY?

IT'S "TOBY."

DID YOU JUST CORRECT ME?

UM...

I ALONE WILL DETERMINE YOUR NAME!!

NOW, WHAT IS YOUR NAME?

TUBBY.

TUBBY, IS IT TRUE THAT YOU'RE SO DUMB THAT YOU...

...SENT YOUR RÉSUMÉ TO THE HUMAN RESOURCES DEPARTMENT?

DO YOU THINK THAT'S WHAT THIS DEPARTMENT DOES? LET ME SHOW YOU WHAT I DO.

I THINK I JUST BECAME AN ENTREPRENEUR.

1/3/99

CATBERT: H.R. DIRECTOR

YOUR CO-WORKERS SAY YOU'RE A SADISTIC NUT.

GIMME FIVE, YOU BIG NUT! AND KEEP UP THE GOOD WORK!

HEY, I'M HAVING A PARTY ON SATURDAY. CAN YOU MAKE IT?

SURE! I'LL BRING MY SPINACH DIP.

DON'T USE THE SHREDDER TODAY.

I RIGGED IT TO KILL OUR NEW SADISTIC NUT CO-WORKER.

WHOA! WHOA!

DOESN'T THAT VOID THE WARRANTY?

I'LL SWITCH SHREDDERS WITH MARKETING TOMORROW.

FROM NOW ON, WE WILL CELEBRATE OUR SERVICE REPS WHO GIVE EXCEPTIONAL CUSTOMER SERVICE.

QUESTION: WHY WOULD WE CELEBRATE EMPLOYEES WHO DO EXTRA WORK WITHOUT GETTING EXTRA PAY?

IT WILL MAKE THEM HAPPY.

CAN WE CELEBRATE THE SMART EMPLOYEES SOME DAY?

I'M WRITING A COMPREHENSIVE "HOW TO" BOOK.

IN CHAPTER ONE, I TEACH PEOPLE HOW TO PICK WINNING LOTTERY NUMBERS.

CHAPTER TWO: HOW TO FIND FREE REAL ESTATE IN VERY NICE NEIGHBORHOODS.

CHAPTER THREE: HOW TO LOSE WEIGHT BY EATING HUGE TUBS OF ICE CREAM.

CHAPTER FOUR: HOW TO BUILD STRONG ABS BY JOINING A GYM AND NEVER GOING.

FINALLY, HOW TO SEE ANGELS BY GIVING YOURSELF A NEAR DEATH EXPERIENCE.

THAT LAST ONE IS JUST TO GET RID OF ALL THE WITNESSES.

ON THE PLUS SIDE, I DON'T FEEL SO BAD ABOUT NOT RECYCLING.

1/10/99 © 1999 United Feature Syndicate, Inc.

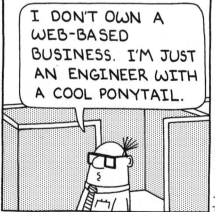

45

46

I USED COMPANY RESOURCES TO BUILD MY OWN INTERNET COMPANY.

APPARENTLY MY LOW JOB SATISFACTION BRED DISLOYALTY, WHICH DRIFTED INTO OUTRIGHT THEFT.

SABOTAGE CAN'T BE FAR AWAY.

WALLY, TELL OUR VIEWERS HOW YOUR INTERNET START-UP GOT SO HOT.

BEATS ME. I WAS WONDERING HOW YOU GOT SO HOT. I'M BURNING UP OVER HERE!

IT SAYS HERE YOU WERE AN ENGINEER.

IS MY PONYTAIL DOING ANYTHING FOR YOU?

I SOLD MY INTERNET BUSINESS AND MARRIED ROXIE.

DON'T WORRY ABOUT MY MONEY. ROXIE INSISTED THAT WE SIGN PRENUPTIAL AGREEMENTS.

NOW FOR OUR HONEY-MOON.

WHOA! THAT'S NOT IN OUR AGREEMENT.

HE DIDN'T READ IT.

2/7/99

DOGBERT'S TECH SUPPORT

FIRST, I NEED TO ASK YOU MANY QUESTIONS.

THEN I WILL TRANSFER YOU TO SOMEONE WHO WILL ASK THE SAME QUESTIONS AGAIN.

WE DO THIS TO REMOVE ANY HOPE YOU MIGHT HAVE HAD THAT WE UNDERSTAND TECHNOLOGY.

DOGBERT'S TECH SUPPORT

I'LL NEED YOUR SERIAL NUMBER, WHICH IS CONVENIENTLY LOCATED INSIDE THE UNIT.

THE STICKER SAYS MY WARRANTY WILL BE VOID IF I OPEN THE CASE.

WELL, CALL ME IF ANYTHING CHANGES.

DO YOU THINK I HAVE TOO MUCH FALSE HUMILITY?

TRY GOING A WEEK WITHOUT USING ANY FALSE HUMILITY, SO I CAN SEE THE DIFFERENCE.

WAKE UP, YOU PIECE OF FETID CARP, AND EXPERIENCE THE JOY OF KNOWING DOGBERT!!

THIS COULD BE A LONG WEEK.

I'D LIKE TO START WITH A CARTOON.

IT'S ABOUT A GUY WHO SHOWS A CARTOON BEFORE GIVING A BORING PRESENTATION.

BUT IT DOESN'T WORK BECAUSE THE CARTOON HAS NO PUNCHLINE.

THIS CONCLUDES MY PRESENTATION. ARE THERE ANY QUESTIONS?

HOW DO I GET THE BOREDOM OUT OF MY HEAD?!!

THE FUNNY THING IS THAT I'LL LIST THIS ON MY ANNUAL ACCOMPLISHMENTS.

AIR! I NEED AIR!!!

I BELIEVE GOD CREATED THE EARTH BECAUSE HE HATES PEOPLE.

AND I BELIEVE COFFEE TASTES BETTER IF YOU STIR IT WITH YOUR FINGER.

IT SOUNDS LIKE A LONELY RELIGION.

THEY ALL START THAT WAY.

68

MY ASTROLOGER TOLD ME TO APPROVE YOUR PROJECT PLAN AS IS.

WHAT?! THAT'S THE CORRECT DECISION. WHAT'S GOING ON HERE?

MY THEORY IS THAT HIS IGNORANCE CLOUDED HIS POOR JUDGMENT.

MY ASTROLOGER TELLS ME THAT SOMEONE HERE IS PLOTTING TO RIP ME OFF.

HOW MUCH IS YOUR ASTROLOGER CHARGING YOU?

ARE YOU PLOTTING TO RIP ME OFF?

I PREFER TO CALL IT HOURLY BILLING.

YESTERDAY YOU TOLD ME TO DO THE EXACT OPPOSITE OF WHAT YOU TOLD ME TODAY.

IT'S MY WAY OF HOLDING YOU ACCOUNTABLE.

I HAVE A VAGUE FEELING THAT I AM NOT BEING ALL THAT I CAN BE.

73

I'M TRYING A LITTLE EXPERIMENT TONIGHT.

I'LL ATTRIBUTE A STUPID OPINION TO YOU...

THEN I'LL AGGRESSIVELY MOCK YOU WHILE YOU SIT THERE SAYING NOTHING.

SO, ACCORDING TO YOU, THE INTERNET IS A PASSING FAD.

YOU MORON! LOOK AROUND YOU! THE INTERNET IS EVERYWHERE!

AND THERE'S NOTHING YOU CAN DO ABOUT IT! NOTHING!!

HOW DID THAT FEEL?

QUITE SATISFYING.

I NEEDED A BACK-UP PLAN IN CASE YOU EVER GET LARYNGITIS.

3|28|99 © 1999 United Feature Syndicate, Inc.

77

...I'M GOING INFRARED FROM THE KEYBOARD TO MY "LINUX" BOX.

NICE, MOM.

I JUST SENT A FLAMEING E-MAIL TO BILL GATES, SAYING, "LINUX RULES!"

YOU WHAT?

LAUNCH THE COMPETITIONKEEPER MISSILES.

DOGBERT, MOM TOLD BILL GATES SHE USES THE "LINUX" OPERATING SYSTEM!

I'M TRACKING FOUR INCOMING MISSILES. I'LL LAUNCH OUR ANTI-MICROSOFT WEAPONS TO INTERCEPT.

I WONDERED WHY A PRESS CONFERENCE WAS BEING HELD ON A HUGE CATAPULT.

LET'S HAVE A LITTLE PREMEETING TO PREPARE FOR THE MEETING TOMORROW.

WHOA! DO YOU THINK IT'S SAFE TO JUMP RIGHT INTO THE PREMEETING WITHOUT PLANNING IT?

OKAY, LET'S GET THIS PRELIMINARY PREMEETING MEETING GOING.

YOU THINK YOU'RE FUNNY, BUT YOU'RE NOT.

OUR ANNUAL ISO 9000 AUDIT IS NEXT WEEK.

WE CAN PASS THE AUDIT IF WE PUT ALL OF OUR NON-CONFORMING DOCUMENTS IN THE TRUNKS OF OUR CARS.

DOESN'T THAT DEFEAT THE PURPOSE OF A VOLUNTARY AUDIT?

AND THEN TORCH THE CARS.

ASOK, I'VE CHOSEN YOU TO PUT OUR BUDGET FORECAST TOGETHER.

IT'S A HARD JOB, BUT YOU'LL GET THE SATISFACTION OF MAKING EVERYONE HATE YOUR TINY GUTS.

MY GUTS ARE NOT TINY.

THE BUDGET CYCLE

AND I'LL NEED A HELICOPTER, DOUBLE ROTOR.

IF YOU HAVE ANY RESPECT FOR ME OR THE BUDGET PROCESS, YOU WILL NOT ASK FOR SUCH OBVIOUS BUDGET PADDING.

AND I'LL NEED THAT CHOPPER FILLED WITH ALBINO TIGER CUBS.

DO YOU HAVE THE BUDGET CALCULATED YET, ASOK?

I NEED TO DOUBLE-CHECK THE NUMBERS.

GIVE ME A COPY NOW. I'LL MENTALLY ADJUST FOR THE POSSIBILITY THE NUMBERS ARE WRONG.

AM I MAKING A HUGE MISTAKE?

THIS SIX IS PROBABLY AN UPSIDE-DOWN NINE.

IT'S A FUNNY THING ABOUT BUDGETS...

NO MATTER HOW HARD YOU TRY, THERE'S ALWAYS A SPREADSHEET ERROR THAT MAKES IT ALL AN EXERCISE IN FUTILITY.

DO YOU MIND IF I HUM?

I DOWNSIZED THE "EASE OF USE" LAB BECAUSE THERE'S NO BUDGET FOR A STAFF.

THEY HAVE A BUDGET. I PUT IT ON THE BACK OF THESE TWO-SIDED PHOTOCOPIES!

WELL, THEY LIVED BY THE SWORD, AND THEY DIED BY THE SWORD.

© 1999 United Feature Syndicate, Inc.

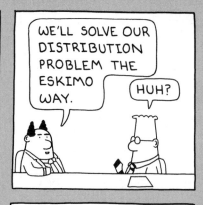

CATBERT: EVIL H.R. DIRECTOR

I'M STARTING AN EMPLOYEE SKILLS DATABASE.

QUESTION: IS THIS THE FIRST STEP IN MOVING EVERYONE TO JOBS THEY DON'T WANT?

NO, NO, NO... THE FIRST STEP WAS WHEN I LAUGHED MYSELF FUZZY THINKING ABOUT IT.

THERE'S BEEN A RASH OF THEFTS FROM CUBICLES.

THE SUSPECT IS DESCRIBED AS FAT AND SLOW-WITTED, WITH POINTY HAIR.

THE BULLETIN STOPS SHORT OF ACTUALLY NAMING HER ALICE.

I USED A HIDDEN CAMERA TO CAPTURE THE THIEF WHO'S BEEN RAIDING OUR CUBICLES.

THE PICTURE IS GRAINY BUT I CAN ALMOST MAKE OUT A HUMAN FORM... OR MAYBE A CAT...

THIS IS OUR MOST RELIABLE COMPUTER, UNLESS YOU TRY TO USE SOFTWARE.

SALE

IT'LL FREEZE SEVERAL TIMES A DAY. BUT YOU CAN RESTART IT BY POKING A SPOON INTO A HOLE IN THE BACK.

HAS THAT EVER WORKED?

WE THINK PEOPLE ARE DOING IT WRONG.

5/6/99 © 1999 United Feature Syndicate, Inc.

CHEST PAINS... MY HEART...

I INVENTED AN ANTIGRAVITY BELT, BUT IT'S HIDDEN!!

5/7/99 © 1999 United Feature Syndicate, Inc.

DO YOU THINK IT'S TRUE?

IT'S WHAT ENGINEERS SAY TO INCREASE THE ODDS OF GETTING CPR.

TINA, I WANT YOU TO WRITE THE CHINESE VERSION OF OUR PRODUCT'S INSTRUCTIONS.

CAN YOU TELL THE DIFFERENCE BETWEEN CHINESE WORDS AND RANDOM SCRIBBLES?

5/8/99 © 1999 United Feature Syndicate, Inc.

NO.

I'LL BE DONE IN FIVE MINUTES.

WALLY, WHAT IS THE QUICKEST WAY TO SEND THESE OLD BINDERS TO THE LANDFILL?

I USUALLY USE "FEDEX." CHARGE IT TO MARKETING; THEY NEVER LOOK AT THEIR EXPENSE REPORTS.

HERE'S ONE MORE THING I CAN NEVER TELL ANYONE ABOUT MY JOB.

WE'LL REDESIGN OUR PROCESSES TO ENABLE ENTERPRISE INTEGRATION OF KNOWLEDGE RESOURCES AND TOOLS.

QUESTION: IS IT OKAY IF I DO NOTHING?

NO.

WELL, EXCUSE ME FOR MAKING A SUGGESTION.

THIS COMPLETES MY PORTION OF THE PROJECT.

THIS PROJECT IS SO WELL-ENGINEERED IT WOULD TAKE A SQUADRON OF IDIOTS TO RUIN IT.

MEANWHILE IN MARKETING

AND WHEN I'M NAPPING, IT IS NOT OKAY TO USE MY EARS AS COASTERS.

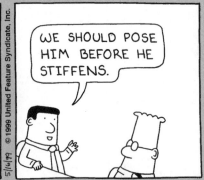

CATBERT: EVIL H.R. DIRECTOR

ASOK, YOU HAVE TAKEN TOO MANY TRAINING CLASSES.

TOO MANY?

YOU'RE TOO SKILLED NOW. THERE'S A RISK YOU'LL LEAVE FOR A BETTER JOB.

DOES THE "SECRET UNTRAINING METHOD" WORK EVERY TIME?

I'VE NEVER TRIED IT BEFORE.

DOGBERT CONSULTS

SPRAY THIS TEFLON^(TM) ON YOUR BODY TO BETTER IGNORE THE INPUT OF YOUR SUBORDINATES.

SPLOIT!

NEXT TIME, SHAKE WELL BEFORE USING.

WHO CARES WHAT YOU SAY?!

THAT'S MY OPINION.

"THAT'S MY OPINION."

NICE TRY, BUT I CAN WIPE IT OFF WITH A DAMP SPONGE !!

THAT'S MY OPINION

THE CORPORATE LAWYER

LET'S PREPARE FOR YOUR COURT TESTIMONY. I'LL PRETEND TO BE THE OTHER SIDE.

LIAR! WHY IS YOUR ATTORNEY SO HANDSOME?

WHAP!

THEY CAN HIT ME?

I DON'T SEE WHY NOT.

CAN YOU EXPLAIN THE MEANING OF THIS INTERNAL E-MAIL MESSAGE?

IT SAYS WE'LL "USE INTEGRATION TOOLS TO LEVERAGE THE UTILITY OF OUR ENTERPRISE-WIDE PROCESSES."

IT APPEARS TO BE SOMETHING WE CALL COMMUNICATION.

PERJURY!

OKAY, WHISTLE-BLOWER, EXPLAIN TO THE JURY THE ALLEGED CRIMES OF YOUR EMPLOYER.

...THEN OUR APPLETS WERE DESIGNED TO CORRUPT COOKIE DATA FROM ALL COMPETING PORTALS.

NICE JURY SELECTION.

SO FAR YOU'VE MADE THEM HUNGRY.

HEH-HEH... I'M USING COMPANY RESOURCES TO E-MAIL MY RÉSUMÉ TO A HEADHUNTER.

IT'S THE PERFECT CRIME.

I'VE GOT MAIL!

I JUST GOT THIS RÉSUMÉ FROM A HEADHUNTER.

EVALUATE HER ENGINEERING SKILLS AND LET ME KNOW IF I SHOULD INTERVIEW HER.

WELL, ALICE, YOU'RE ALMOST QUALIFIED TO WORK HERE, BUT I'M CONCERNED ABOUT YOUR LOYALTY.

I'LL WEAR A CLEVER DISGUISE THEN INTERVIEW FOR THE ENGINEERING JOB HERE.

IF HE OFFERS ME MORE MONEY THAN I MAKE NOW, I'LL TAKE THE JOB.

HEH-HEH.

YOU'RE SUSPICIOUSLY FASHIONABLE FOR AN ENGINEER.

I STORE TOOLS UP THERE.

CATBERT: EVIL DIRECTOR OF HUMAN RESOURCES

I HIRED A NEW ENGINEER FOR YOUR PROJECT.

HE'S NEVER BEEN AN ENGINEER BEFORE.

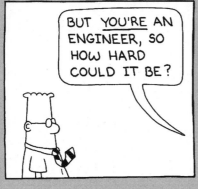

BUT YOU'RE AN ENGINEER, SO HOW HARD COULD IT BE?

AND HE'S CHEAP! I'LL GET A HUGE RAISE FOR BEING UNDER BUDGET.

AND YOUR PROJECT WILL FAIL! HA HA HA HA!

UH-OH. I LAUGHED MYSELF FULL OF STATIC ELECTRICITY.

FUZZY. CUTE.

ZAP!

HE'S DEAD. NOW WHAT?

I GUESS YOU'LL HAVE TO DRAG HIM TO MEETINGS.

I'M EXILED TO THE QUALITY ASSURANCE DEPARTMENT. MY CAREER IS DOOMED.

I CAN'T LET MY OLD DEPARTMENT FORGET ME. THEY'RE MY ONLY HOPE OF RETURNING TO ENGINEERING.

IT MUST BE BREAK TIME IN THE Q.A. DEPARTMENT.

I'LL GET THE FIRE HOSE.

ASOK! DID YOU ESCAPE YOUR JOB AT QUALITY ASSURANCE?

YES. I HAD TO TAKE A JOB AS A SECRETARY'S ASSISTANT. I'LL WORK MY WAY BACK UP TO INTERN.

IT'S FOUR O'CLOCK. CALL MY KIDS AND YELL AT THEM.

CURSING OR NO CURSING?

CATBERT: EVIL H.R. DIRECTOR

I WILL NOW USE THE SCIENCE OF FACE-READING TO DETERMINE YOUR POTENTIAL.

I SEE YOUR FACE RIDING PROUDLY ATOP A MIGHTY THOROUGHBRED HORSE.

JOCKEY?

SADDLE.

WHAT'S YOUR NEW MANAGEMENT BOOK ABOUT?

IT'S A BUNCH OF OBVIOUS ADVICE PACKAGED WITH QUOTES FROM FAMOUS DEAD PEOPLE.

DID GANDHI REALLY SAY "GET THAT #!¢3% DESSERT CART OFF OF MY FOOT!"?

HE MIGHT HAVE.

DOGBERT GETS A LOAN

I PLAN TO BUY ALL THE COPIES OF A BOOK I AUTHORED, THUS MAKING IT A BESTSELLER.

AND I'D LIKE TO USE YOUR HOUSE AS COLLATERAL.

UNLESS IT'S A DUMP.

HOW ARE YOU PLANNING TO PAY US BACK?

DO YOU TAKE BOOKS?

DOGBERT IN HOLLYWOOD

I'D LIKE TO TURN YOUR BOOK INTO A MOVIE.

WE HAVE TO KEEP IT REAL, SO ANY NORMAL PERSON CAN RELATE TO IT.

DO YOU KNOW ANY NORMAL PEOPLE?

NO, BUT I'M WILLING TO WATCH MOVIES TO LEARN ABOUT THEM.

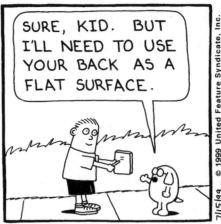

THE FENG SHUI CONSULTANT

THIS OFFICE IS SWARMING WITH EVIL SPIRITS.

IT IS?

THERE'S ONE IN YOUR VENT!

OOH — HE DUCKED BACK IN BEFORE YOU SAW HIM.

PUT RUBBER BANDS AROUND YOUR PANT LEGS TO KEEP THE SPIRITS OUT OF YOUR TROUSERS.

I FIGURE THE EVIL SPIRITS WILL MOUNT A REAR ASSAULT THROUGH THAT WINDOW.

AAAGH!

WHAT DID YOU SEE?!!

IT'S GONE NOW.

YOUR ONLY HOPE IS TO TURN YOUR SECRETARY'S CUBICLE INTO A KOI POND.

DO YOU FEEL ANY LUCKIER?

**#! @%☼

CATBERT: EVIL H.R. DIRECTOR